My Dog, Dom

By Cameron Macintosh

Dom the dog
is on the rug.

Dom is a big dog.

He was a big pup!

Dom can not run,
but he is not sad.

Dom can get in the mud.

He has fun in the mud!

Dom can dig in the pit.

Dig, dig, dig!

Dom can sit in the pit.

I hug Dom in the pit.

Dom gets on his bed
for a nap.

I pat Dom.

Dom is my pet.

CHECKING FOR MEANING

1. What are three things Dom does when he is outside? *(Literal)*

2. What does Dom do on his bed? *(Literal)*

3. Why do you think Dom can not run? *(Inferential)*

EXTENDING VOCABULARY

rug	What is a *rug*? What is another word that has a similar meaning? Which sounds are in this other word?
sad	What does *sad* mean? How do you feel if you are not *sad*? Explain that these words are opposite in meaning. Talk about other words that are opposites, e.g. hot – cold; big – little; on – off; up – down.
fun	Look at the word *fun*. What word would you make if you took away the *f* and put an *r* at the beginning?

MOVING BEYOND THE TEXT

1. Why are dogs good pets?

2. What do we need to do to care for a dog?

3. Why do dogs like being outside?

4. How do you know the boy in the story likes Dom?

SPEED SOUNDS

Dd	Jj	Oo	Gg	Uu
Cc	Bb	Rr	Ee	Ff	Hh	Nn
Mm	Ss	Aa	Pp	Ii	Tt

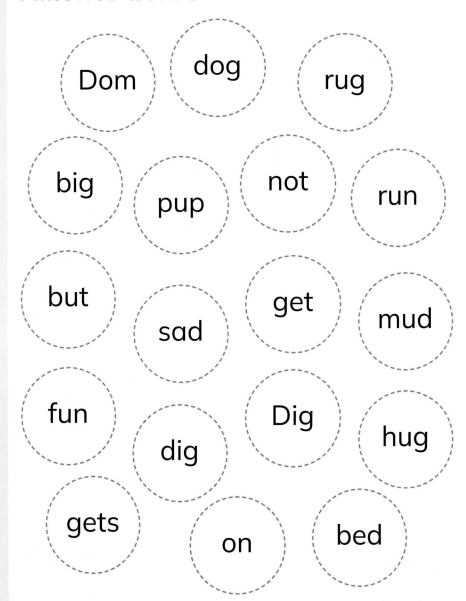

Dom

dog

rug

big

pup

not

run

but

sad

get

mud

fun

dig

Dig

hug

gets

on

bed